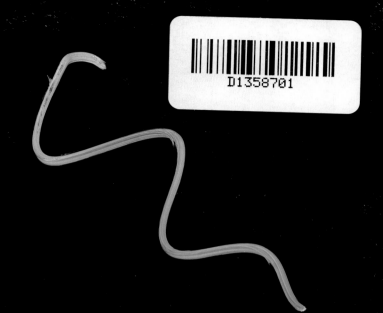

LOOK INTO SPACE

STARS
AND
GALAXIES

Jon Kirkwood

COPPER BEECH BOOKS
BROOKFIELD, CONNECTICUT

© Aladdin Books Ltd 1999
Produced by
Aladdin Books Ltd
28 Percy Street
London W1P 0LD

First published in the United States
in 1999 by
Copper Beech Books,
an imprint of
The Millbrook Press
2 Old New Milford Road
Brookfield, Connecticut 06804

Editor: Jon Richards

Design
David West Children's Book Design

Designer: Simon Morse

Illustrator: Ian Thompson

Picture research: Brooks Krikler Research

Printed in Belgium

Cataloging-in-Publication Data is on file at
the Library of Congress.

ISBN 0-7613-0917-9 (lib. bdg.)

5 4 3 2 1

CONTENTS

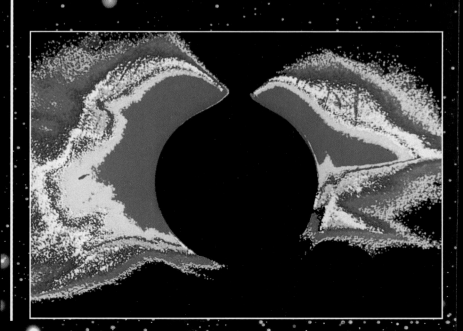

INTRODUCTION

Have you ever wondered what lies in space, beyond the comfort of the earth? *Stars and Galaxies* will take you on a tour of the heavens, looking at the objects that shine in the night sky — all from the comfort of your armchair.

Starting with the sun, the book looks at what makes stars shine and what happens to them during their lifetimes. It also examines different types of stars, including black holes, white dwarfs, and red supergiants. Finally the book takes a look into the very distant future to find out how the universe might end!

CHESTNUT HILL

EXCELLENT EXPERIMENTS
Wherever you see this symbol (*below*), you'll find an experiment that you can do. Just follow the easy-to-understand instructions, and the results will open your eyes to the wonders of space. Find out why the sun is hot and where you can see our nearest galaxy in the night sky.

OUR STAR

Shining brightly on a sunny day (*right*), the sun is the most important object in the sky. As well as lighting and heating the earth, it is the center of the solar system, with the planets and other objects orbiting it. Like the stars we see twinkling in the night sky, the sun is a star. However, because these stars are very far away, they appear very dim compared to the bright sun.

MOONSHINE

Our moon (*left*) and the other planets we see in the night sky do not give out their own light. Instead, they reflect the light of the sun. The moon is so bright because it is close to the earth.

STAR POWER

We can feel the energy of the sun as warmth on our skin on a sunny day. We can use this energy in many ways. For instance, there are a number of solar furnaces (*left*) where the energy from the sun is gathered and concentrated so it can heat up water to make steam. This steam then drives a turbine, which spins a dynamo to make electricity.

ENERGY WE EAT

Plants and animals depend on the sun for energy. Plants take the energy from sunlight and use it in a process called photosynthesis to make nutrients to help them grow. When we eat plants, such as corn and wheat (*below*), our bodies break down these nutrients, providing the energy, helping us to move, grow, and live our lives.

SUN FACTS AND FIGURES

Distance from Earth —
93 million miles
(150 million km)
Diameter — 865,000 miles
(1.39 million km)
Age — 4.5 billion years
Surface temperature — 11,000°F
(6,000°C)

WARNING: never look directly at the sun. It can blind you!

THE COLOR OF SUNLIGHT

Although sunlight appears white, it is actually made up of different colors that, when added together, make white. You can see the colors that make up the sun's white light by splitting it up with a

piece of glass called a prism (*above*). The colors you'll see are red, orange, yellow, green, blue, indigo, and violet. The same thing happens when sunlight is split up by the grooves on a compact disk, creating a rainbow effect on the disk's surface (*left*). Scientists can split up the light from a distant star into a spectrum. This will tell them more about that star (*see* pages 20-21).

INSIDE THE SUN

Like all stars, the sun is a huge ball of gas that is being held together and squeezed by its own gravity. The pressure makes some gas atoms fuse together, releasing enormous amounts of energy in a process called nuclear fusion. This release of energy is what makes the sun shine brightly.

Convection zone

Radiative zone

Core

Protons

Deuterium nuclei

Nuclear fusion takes place at the sun's core (above). The photons that are released (see right) travel through the next layer of the sun called the radiative zone. From here, huge gas currents swirl in circles in the convection zone, carrying energy to the sun's surface. This energy is then released into space as radiation to warm the planets.

THE SUN BOMB

The most destructive single man-made event is the detonation of a hydrogen bomb (*above*). The reaction in a hydrogen bomb is similar to the nuclear fusion process at the sun's core. However, the sun releases millions of times more energy than the most powerful hydrogen bomb every second!

PLANET OR STAR?

Like the sun, Jupiter (*right*) is a huge ball of gas. The giant planet also gives out more heat than it receives from the sun. At one

time it was thought that there might be nuclear fusion taking place in its core. It is now known that the planet is too small for the temperatures and pressures at its core to be high enough for fusion to start. Because of this, Jupiter remains a planet and is not a star.

AMAZING SUN FACTS

700 million tons of hydrogen are converted into helium every second.
The sun puts out some 386 billion billion megawatts of power.
The pressure at the sun's core is 250 billion times that at sea level on Earth.
The temperature at the sun's core is 27 million°F (15 million°C).
Light takes 8.3 minutes to travel between the sun and the earth.

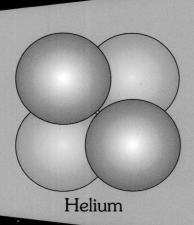

Helium

In the sun's core, tiny hydrogen atom nuclei, called protons (left), come together to form a heavy hydrogen nucleus called deuterium.

Because of the high pressures, two of these deuterium nuclei are fused together to form helium. One result of this fusion is the release of packets of energy called photons.

Photon

A LOT OF HOT AIR

One of the reasons why it is so hot at the center of the sun is because the gases at its core are being squeezed together by gravity. To see how compressing a gas can heat it up, place your thumb over the end of a bicycle pump and pump as hard as you can (*right*). You will feel your thumb heat up as you try to squeeze the gas in the pump. As the molecules of air are compressed, they rub together more often, releasing more energy as heat and warming your thumb. However, you will not be able to squeeze hard enough for nuclear fusion to start!

SURFACE OF THE SUN

The part of the sun that makes up its shining disk is called the photosphere. It might seem hard to believe, but the sun is not a uniform bright disk. Observed in safety (*see right*) and by professional astronomers, it shows up many surface features. Under certain conditions, the sun's surface appears covered in small granules (*right*) or blotched by dark sunspots.

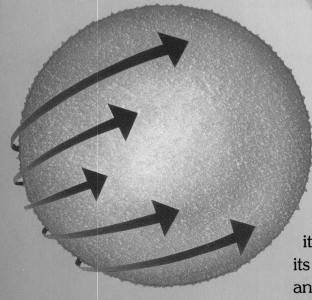

IN A SPIN
Astronomers have found that the sun does not spin at the same rate across its surface. It spins more slowly at its equator than at its poles — it takes 37 days to rotate at the equator and only 26 toward the poles (*left*). This is because the sun is not a solid body like the earth, but a ball of gas.

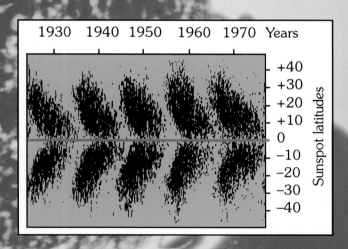

SPOTS AND BUTTERFLIES

Sunspots (*left*) are regions where the temperature is a little cooler than the rest of the surface. Spots usually come in pairs, and they also appear more often at certain times. The spots usually appear in cycles that are 11 years long.

These cycles can be seen in a chart that shows the appearance of spots at different latitudes over time. It looks like a series of butterfly wings (*below*).

SPOT WATCH

The <u>only</u> safe way to observe the disk of the sun is to project its image onto a piece of white cardboard, using a telescope (*below*). You might be able to see some sunspots on the surface. Over the course of a few days, these spots will move over the face of the sun as it rotates. Spots can last from a couple of days to several months.

1930	1940	1950	1960	1970	Years

Sunspot latitudes: +40, +30, +20, +10, 0, −10, −20, −30, −40

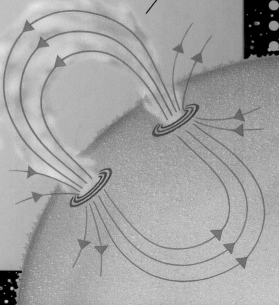

Solar prominence

MAGNETIC SPOTS

Sunspots have magnetic fields associated with them. Plumes of hot gas, called solar prominences, erupt from the sun's surface, following the lines of magnetic force that link a pair of sunspots (*right*).

The granules that cover the sun (above) are, in fact, currents of hot gas rising to the surface (see pages 6-7).

AROUND THE SUN

Beyond its surface, or photosphere, the sun has an atmosphere of hot gases. This atmosphere is made up of two regions, the chromosphere and the corona. The corona ejects a stream of particles called the solar wind. The sun has other atmospheric features, including prominences.

CORONA

The corona is the outermost part of the sun's atmosphere. It is relatively dim and can only really be observed when there is a total solar eclipse. During this time, it can be seen as a glowing halo (*above*). When the image is color-coded (*above left*), it shows that the brightest part of the corona is closest to the sun.

PROMINENCE

Prominences often look like flaming arches and are made of glowing gas (*right*). Some prominences are short lived, emerging quickly and subsiding within minutes or hours. Others live longer and can last for several months.

SOLAR WIND

The high temperature of the corona causes particles to fly off into space. This stream of particles, called the solar wind, shoots out from the corona in a similar pattern to a shower of water from a rotary garden sprinkler (*right*). The solar wind "blows" out through the solar system, going beyond all of the planets.

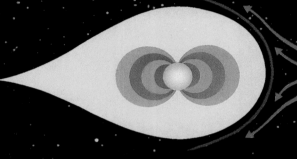

MAGNETIC FIELD

The sun has a strong magnetic field (*above*), which is similar to, but much larger than, the earth's magnetic field. The sun's magnetic field interacts with interstellar gases that the sun passes through as it moves through space.

SPICULES

The lower part of the sun's atmosphere is called the chromosphere. Inside the chromosphere are spicules, long flamelike structures (*left*). These accelerate upward from the surface of the sun at speeds of around 62,000 mph (100,000 km/h). Individual spicules can be up to 6,200 miles (10,000 km) long.

SOLAR FLARES

A solar flare is a sudden brightening of the chromosphere. Some solar flares give off so much radiation that their effects can be felt as magnetic storms on earth. These storms can affect radio transmissions and even cause power line failures.

OTHER STARS

The sun is not the only star in space. You should be able to see thousands of stars in the night sky using just your eyes. Each of these is a huge glowing ball of gas, like the sun. But they only appear as small pinpricks of light because they lie so very far away. However, we can only see a tiny fraction of the billions of stars in our galaxy.

SEEING STARS
Because telescopes and binoculars collect more light than your eyes, they are extremely useful for looking at dim and distant objects, such as stars. Look at the sky on a clear night, and you will find that you can see many more stars using a telescope or a pair of binoculars than you can with the naked eye (*above*).

STAR NEIGHBORS
Stars are so far away that we use the distance light travels in a year to measure the distances to them. One light-year is 5.9 million million miles (9.6 million million km).

0 light-years		5 light-years
Sun	Proxima Centauri	Barnard's Star
0.00001 light-years	4.2 light-years	6 light-years

FINDING THE DISTANCE

With the help of accurate measuring devices, astronomers have calculated the distance to many nearby stars using the parallax method. Measuring the change in position of the star when the earth reaches opposite ends of its orbit allows the distance of the star to be figured out using simple geometry (*right*). You can see how this works by pointing your thumb at a distant object and then alternately opening and closing each eye. The object will appear to move in relation to your thumb (*left*).

Star

Sun

Earth

The Big Dipper

100,000 years ago

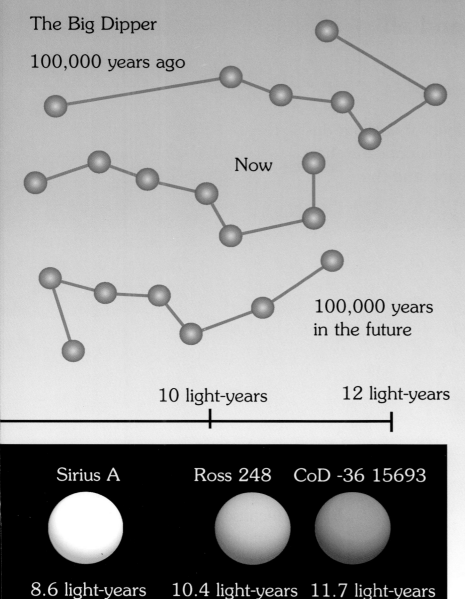

Now

100,000 years in the future

10 light-years

12 light-years

Sirius A

Ross 248

CoD -36 15693

8.6 light-years

10.4 light-years

11.7 light-years

STARS IN MOTION

The stars might seem to be still in the night sky, just hanging there in their fixed positions relative to each other for year after year. But if they are watched very carefully, and their positions measured extremely accurately over time, some, especially some of the closer ones, can be seen to be moving. This movement is called a star's proper motion and is caused by the fact that the stars are not all drifting through space (orbiting the galaxy) in quite the same direction or with the same speed. Over time, many constellations will change shape because of the proper motions of stars. For instance, the Big Dipper was very different 100,000 years ago and will look very different in 100,000 years' time (*above left*).

A STAR IS BORN

Our star has been around for a very long time, but it has not always been there. In fact, it came into being some 4.5 billion years ago. Before that, it was a cloud of gas and dust that was shrinking under the force of its own gravity. From this, formed the sun and all of its planets.

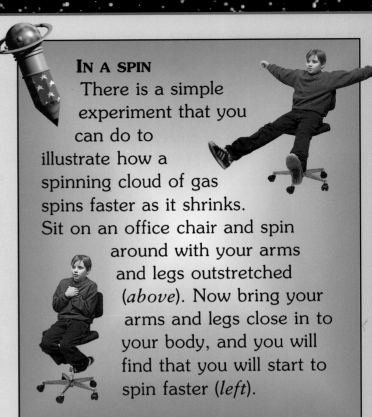

IN A SPIN
There is a simple experiment that you can do to illustrate how a spinning cloud of gas spins faster as it shrinks. Sit on an office chair and spin around with your arms and legs outstretched (*above*). Now bring your arms and legs close in to your body, and you will find that you will start to spin faster (*left*).

1 FROM A CLOUD
A concentration of mass in a cloud of gas and dust started the process of collapse. This concentration attracted matter to itself by gravity, and the whole cloud started to fall in on itself. As it started to shrink, the cloud began to spin.

3

3 GETTING HOTTER
Gas and dust were pulled in to the center. As they rushed toward the center, they banged into each other, causing the temperature to rise.

2

2 SHRINKING CLOUD
As the cloud collapsed more and more, it spun faster and faster (*see activity above*). Because it was spinning, it flattened out until a disk formed around a central core to form what is called a solar nebula. The planets eventually formed from this solar nebula.

1

4 GAS PLUMES

At some point, much of the gas and dust from the spinning cloud was ejected in huge plumes above and below the forming star. These plumes formed at the poles of this star because matter escaping from here was not blocked by the rest of the spinning disk of dust and gas. About one-fifth of the gas and dust from the original shrinking cloud was lost during this process.

4

5

5 FUSION STARTS

The pressure and temperature in the center of the cloud eventually became so great that the atoms there started to fuse (*see* pages 6-7), releasing enormous amounts of energy, and the star started to shine.

Mercury

Venus

Mars

Earth

ROCKY BODIES

The sun is not very old by cosmic standards. One consequence of this is the fact that it can have planets made up of rock and metal, like the earth. These materials were actually made in other stars, which exploded, throwing these materials into clouds from which new stars formed. Only second-generation stars, like the sun, can have planets not made wholly of gas.

LIFE CYCLE OF STARS

Once a star is born from a cloud of gas that has collapsed, it goes through a phase where it shines relatively steadily. In the case of our star, the sun, this phase has already lasted some 4.5 billion years and will last another 4 or 5 billion years. After this period, stars exhaust their fuel and, depending on how massive they were to begin with, die in one of a number of ways.

SMALL STARS

Stars that are much smaller than the sun — with about 0.06 times the mass of the sun — might glow dimly as small brown stars called brown dwarfs. They burn for a very long time before cooling and fading away to become stellar remnants called black dwarfs (*left*).

STARS LIKE THE SUN

A star that is about the same size as the sun will burn for about 10 billion years. Then, once the fuel in its core starts to get low, the star will start to swell until it is the size of a red giant star (*below*).

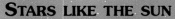

Star expands   Red giant

BIG STARS

Really big stars "burn up" very quickly — sometimes lasting only 20 million years. When they have used up all their fuel, they swell to an enormous size and explode in a huge explosion called a supernova. Left behind are tiny, rapidly spinning neutron stars (which send out powerful beams of radio pulses) or even, in the case of the biggest stars, black holes (*see* pages 22-23).

Beam of radio waves

FLASHING STARS

As neutron stars spin in space, their beams of radio waves sweep the sky. Watching them from one spot, it would appear as if they were pulsing as each beam swept past. You can recreate this effect by spinning a flashlight on a flat surface and watching as the light appears to flash on and off.

DEATH OF THE INNER PLANETS

In 4 or 5 billion years' time, when the sun is very much older than it is now, it will have used up the fuel in its core and will swell into a red giant star, many times its current size. Estimates of this size vary, but it will almost certainly swallow the orbit of Mercury and might reach out to be as wide as the orbit of Earth, or even wider toward the orbit of Mars (*below*). Life on the inner planets would be impossible long before this happened, and when the sun gets this large, the rocky inner worlds will be incinerated.

Once all of the fuel has been burned up, the core of the star will collapse, throwing off the star's outer layers to create a ring-shaped cloud of debris called a planetary nebula.

White dwarf

Meanwhile, the core collapses down to a white dwarf, a brightly glowing but tiny object, where matter is packed in so densely that a teaspoonful weighs many tons.

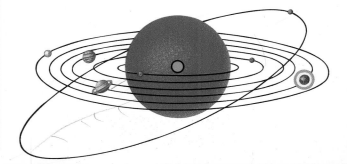

BRIGHTNESS OF STARS

Objects in the sky do not shine with the same intensity — some are brighter than others. Their brightness is affected by two factors: how luminous they are and how far away they are. Astronomers use two scales to measure a star's brightness — its apparent magnitude (how bright it appears from earth) and its absolute magnitude (how much light the star is actually putting out).

ORION AS WE SEE IT

One of the most prominent constellations is Orion (*right*). It has several stars that seem bright to us. But the brightness of these stars as seen from earth is not a true representation of their actual light output. Some of the stars have very high actual light outputs, but seem less bright because they are farther away than others in the sky that have lower light outputs.

Vega 0.03

Polaris 2

Spica 1

Sirius −1.46

APPARENT MAGNITUDE

The brightness of an object in the sky is called its apparent magnitude. Shown on this page (*left and above*) are some of the brighter objects in the sky with their magnitude numbers — the lower the number, the brighter the object in the sky. Their size represents their apparent magnitude — the bigger they are, the brighter they appear in the sky.

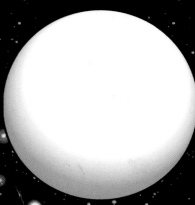

Venus −4

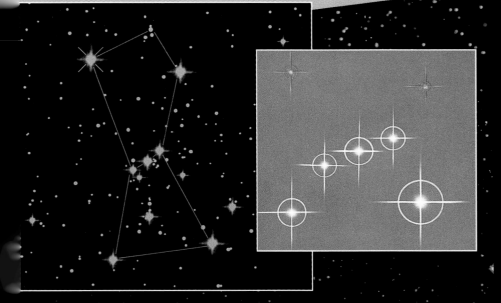

ABSOLUTE MAGNITUDE

To measure a star's actual light output, astronomers figure out its absolute magnitude. This compares the light output of stars as if they were seen from the same distance. The chart (*left*) shows how Orion would appear when the stars are represented by their absolute magnitudes.

FAR-SEEING HUBBLE

Above the haze of the atmosphere, the Hubble Space Telescope (*right*) can see very dim objects. For example, it can detect stars of apparent magnitude 29. This is more than 1.5 billion times fainter than stars that we can see with the naked eye.

8 BRIGHTEST STARS

Sirius (Canis Major)
8.6 light-years away
Apparent magnitude −1.46
Canopus (Carina)
74 light-years away
Apparent magnitude −0.72
Rigil Kentaurus (Centaurus)
4.3 light-years away
Apparent magnitude −0.27
Arcturus (Boötes)
34 light-years away
Apparent magnitude −0.04
Vega (Lyra)
25 light-years away
Apparent magnitude 0.03
Capella (Auriga)
41 light-years away
Apparent magnitude 0.08
Rigel (Orion)
1,400 light-years away
Apparent magnitude 0.12
Procyon (Canis Minor)
11.4 light-years away
Apparent magnitude 0.38

GETTING FAINTER

At night, get some friends to hold identical flashlights at different distances away from you (*right*). You will see how the flashlights that are farther away appear dimmer. Astronomers use this principle to work out how far away stars are. Given two similar stars, the dimmer one will be the more distant.

COLORS OF STARS

Look carefully at the stars and you will see that they come in many colors. These colors can tell us a star's size and how hot it burns. Scientists can split up a star's light into a spectrum. This spectrum also contains black lines, called absorption lines. These lines are caused by elements in the star blocking out certain colors of light. From this spectrum and the pattern of absorption lines, scientists figure out what type of star it is.

BRIGHT BLUE STARS

The spectrum of a blue star has few absorption lines (*below*). This type of star burns hotter and brighter than other stars. As a result, they burn up their fuel very quickly and do not live for very long. These stars tend to be quite large — about 20 times the diameter of our own sun.

Blue star

Yellow-white star

ORDINARY YELLOW-WHITE STARS

A star like our sun is a yellow-white color (*left*). The spectrum of a yellow-white star contains more absorption lines than a blue star. Yellow-white stars can burn for 10 billion years before they swell up and die.

Red star

SMALL RED STARS

Small red stars, smaller than our sun, are much cooler than both yellow-white and blue stars. Their surface temperature is only about 6,300°F (3,500°C) — blue stars have a surface temperature of up to 45,000°F (25,000°C)! Red stars can burn for a very long time — up to 100 billion years! The spectrum of a red star contains a lot of absorption lines (*right*).

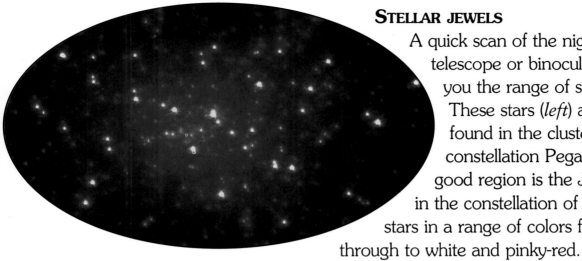

STELLAR JEWELS

A quick scan of the night sky with a telescope or binoculars will show you the range of star colors. These stars (*left*) are blue stars found in the cluster M15 in the constellation Pegasus. Another good region is the Jewel Box cluster in the constellation of Crux. It contains stars in a range of colors from blue through to white and pinky-red.

CHARTING THE COLORS

Astronomers have found that there is a relationship between different star characteristics, including surface temperature, absolute magnitude, and color. For example, blue stars shine very brightly and are very hot, while small red stars are very dim and quite cool in comparison. Astronomers can plot these characteristics and map the different types of stars using a graph known as the Hertzsprung-Russell diagram (*right* and *below right*).

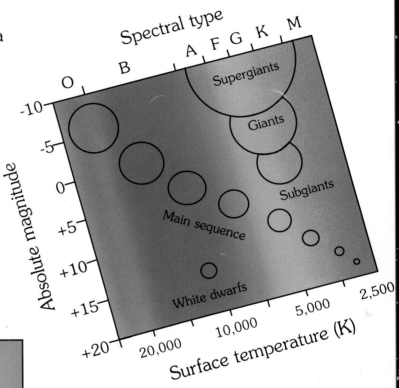

COMPARING STARS

To get an idea of the size of different stars imagine that our sun was the size of a Ping-Pong ball. A tiny white dwarf star would be a small sphere less than 0.16 in (4 mm) across. A blue star would be about 31 in (80 cm) across (about the size of a beach ball), while a giant red star would be a sphere about 79 ft (24 m) across!

THE HERTZSPRUNG-RUSSELL DIAGRAM

When mapped on the Hertzsprung-Russell diagram, stars fall into zones (*above*). Those which fall in the diagonal band across the chart are stars that are shining steadily. They are called main-sequence stars. Those above this band are at the end of their lives and are swelling into giants and supergiants. Those below are also at the end of their lives, but have become white dwarf stars.

BLACK HOLES

When a really massive star reaches the end of its life, it swells into a red supergiant star and explodes in a supernova. What's left of the core collapses in on itself to form a black hole. This is a region of space where the gravity is so strong that even light cannot escape its powerful pull.

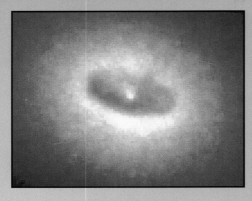

BLACK HOLE SPOTTING

Because light cannot escape from black holes, they cannot actually be seen! Instead, astronomers can detect them by the way they affect other objects near to them. This image (*above*) shows a disk of gas at the center of a distant galaxy that astronomers have found is giving off large amounts of high-energy radiation, such as X rays. Astronomers believe that these X rays are being emitted by the gas because it is being heated as it is sucked in by the immense gravity of a black hole.

IN FOR A STRETCH

A person who got too close to a black hole would be spaghettified — stretched out and pulled apart by the immense gravity field (*left*). The stretching force would be the same as having 8.5 million people attached to your ankles while you hang onto a bar here on earth! Black holes also distort the effects of time around them. As the person approached the black hole, the universe would appear to speed up, while another person, watching from a safe distance, would see the first person appear to slow down.

Gravity well

Black hole

DEFORMING SPACE

You can visualize the effects of gravity by imagining the universe is a flat plane. Stars deform that plane with their mass, creating dips known as "gravity wells." The more mass the object has, the larger the well. A black hole, which has infinite mass, would have a gravity well without a bottom (*right*).

BACK TO THE PAST

Because black holes distort time and space around them, some scientists believe that they could be used to travel backward and forward through time. Huge problems must be overcome in creating the technology that would make this safe and predictable. Otherwise any prospective time travelers would be torn apart or emerge at a totally unwanted destination (*below*).

GRAVITY WELL

You can make a gravity well like that around a massive object by stretching some plastic food wrap evenly across a bowl. Put a heavy object, such as a golf ball, on the food wrap. It will stretch the food wrap, creating a depression similar to the gravity well created by a star. Now roll another lighter object, like a marble, onto the food wrap so that it misses the golf ball. The path of the marble will be bent toward the golf ball, just as the gravity of a large object in space attracts smaller ones.

STAR CLUSTERS

Stars are not evenly scattered across the sky. In many regions of space, there are clumps of stars — some of these clumps may contain thousands of stars. These clumps are called clusters. There are two types of clusters: galactic, or open clusters, and larger globular clusters, which hang around the edges of galaxies.

LOOKING AT CLUSTERS

Some open clusters can be seen with the naked eye. One of the easiest to find is the Pleiades cluster (*above*) in the constellation of Taurus. The brightest stars in the cluster are the Seven Sisters, all of which can be seen unaided. The cluster does, however, contain several hundred stars.

DENSE CLUSTER

This image (*left*) was taken by the Hubble Space Telescope. Previous images of this cluster, known as NGC 1850, showed less than 1,000 stars. Hubble's clearer vision, however, picked out nearly 10,000 stars (that's more than twice the number of stars you can see in the entire sky with the naked eye!). The cluster lies 166,000 light-years away and can be found in the constellation of Doradus.

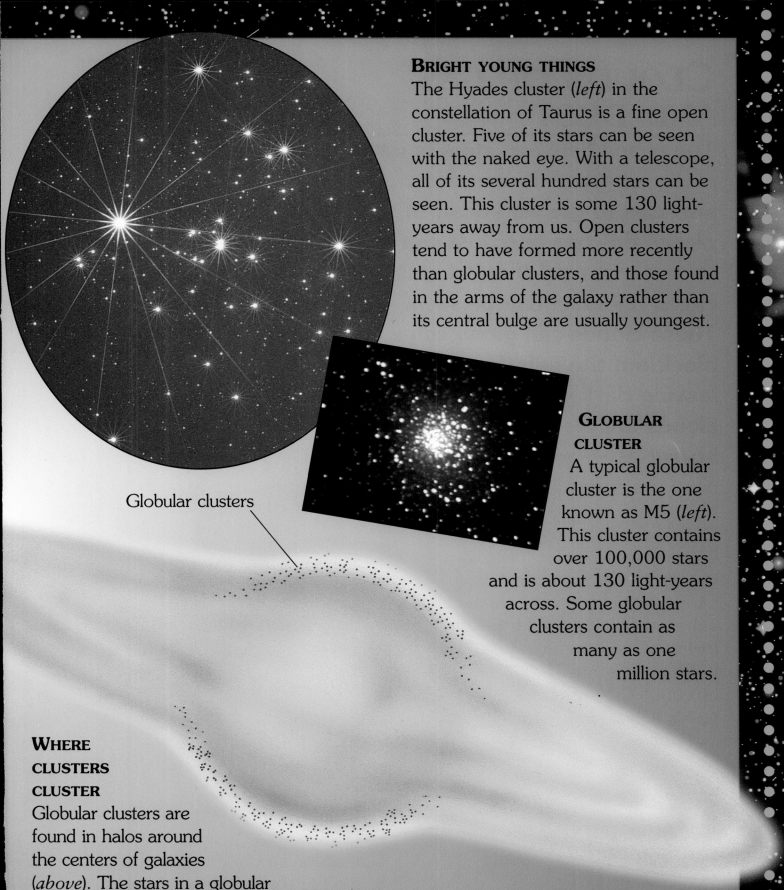

BRIGHT YOUNG THINGS

The Hyades cluster (*left*) in the constellation of Taurus is a fine open cluster. Five of its stars can be seen with the naked eye. With a telescope, all of its several hundred stars can be seen. This cluster is some 130 light-years away from us. Open clusters tend to have formed more recently than globular clusters, and those found in the arms of the galaxy rather than its central bulge are usually youngest.

GLOBULAR CLUSTER

A typical globular cluster is the one known as M5 (*left*). This cluster contains over 100,000 stars and is about 130 light-years across. Some globular clusters contain as many as one million stars.

Globular clusters

WHERE CLUSTERS CLUSTER

Globular clusters are found in halos around the centers of galaxies (*above*). The stars in a globular cluster are held together in a ball by their own mutual gravity, and the cluster as a whole is in orbit around a galaxy's center. A typical globular cluster takes some 100 million years to complete an orbit around a galaxy.

Our own galaxy has some 140 globular clusters scattered around its fringes (above).

CLOUDS OF GAS AND DUST

The space between stars is never really empty — it contains particles of gas and dust. In some places this gas and dust can be so concentrated that "clouds," called nebulae, can be seen. These clouds can glow, shine, or block out the light from stars, leaving dark patches. Many clouds are also stellar nurseries — regions where new stars are being born.

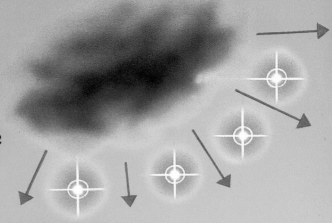

SHINING CLOUDS

So-called reflection nebulae shine by the light they reflect from nearby stars (*above*). These nebulae are often the site of the birth of stars (*see right*).

GLOWING CLOUDS

Glowing nebulae glow because the gas in them is heated by ultraviolet radiation from stars either within the cloud or nearby (*below*). They are heated so much — to some 18,000°F (10,000° C) — that they give out visible light, usually red light.

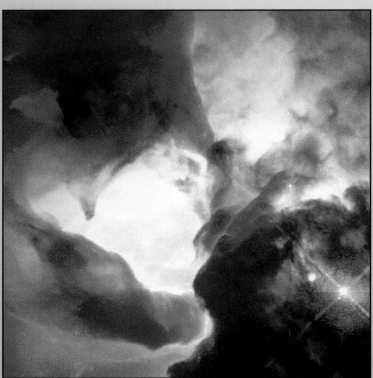

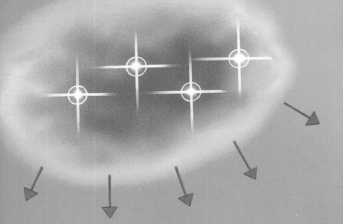

LAGOON NEBULA

The Lagoon nebula (*above*) can be found in the constellation of Sagittarius. Much of this cloud of gas and dust is glowing due to the warming effects of nearby stars. However, other parts of the cloud block out some of the light, giving the nebula its lagoonlike appearance.

EAGLE NEBULA

The Eagle nebula (*below*), or NGC 6611 (part of it is also known as M16), is a cloud of gas and dust some 7,000 light-years away. Inside the long fingers of the cloud, gas gathers into blobs that, due to the effects of gravity, start to contract. As they contract, they heat up until the cloud ignites and becomes a star. The nebula glows because it is heated up by the birth of these stars.

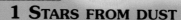

1 STARS FROM DUST

Astronomers think the birth of some stars may begin with the explosion of another, which sends shock waves into a nearby nebula.

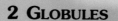

2 GLOBULES

The shock waves cause matter in the nebula to clump together into concentrated areas called Bok globules.

3 STARS IGNITE

These globules contract under the force of their own gravity. After some time, nuclear fusion occurs, and the stars start to shine.

SWEEPING UP NEW STARS

As the shock waves travel through a cloud of gas and dust, they push the particles together to form the Bok globules. You can see how this occurs by pushing a broom or brush through some dust or sand. As the brush moves forward, dust collects in front of it in a concentrated area.

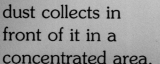

GALAXIES

Galaxies are huge collections of stars. Our galaxy, also called the Milky Way, is quite a large one. It is thought to have as many as 100 billion stars in it, and measures nearly 100,000 light-years across and 1,000 light-years thick! These enormous star cities are held together by the gravity of all the objects within them.

LOOK AT THE MILKY WAY

On a really clear night when the moon is not out, look up into the sky, and you will see the Milky Way (*above*). This milky band is our view of our own galaxy. The Milky Way is, in fact, a spiral-shaped disk, and this band is our edge-on view. Its milky appearance is the light from billions of stars blending together.

ANDROMEDA GALAXY

The closest comparable galaxy to our own is the galaxy in Andromeda (*above*). It's about two or three times the mass of the Milky Way and a spiral galaxy, like our own. However, because we see it from the side, it's hard to spot its spiral structure. At 2.3 million light-years away, it is the most distant object visible with the naked eye.

LOOK FOR ANDROMEDA

When it's good and dark, you might be able to see the galaxy in the constellation of Andromeda (*below*). Good months to see it in the Northern Hemisphere are October and November when it will be high in the sky at about ten P.M. You should be able to see it as a pearly pool of light with the naked eye.

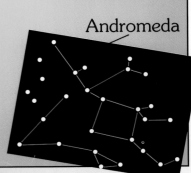

Andromeda

1 GALAXY FORMATION

Like stars, galaxies form from clouds of gas that collapse under their own force of gravity, spinning as they do so. At first, stars form only in the center of the huge cloud. Many of these stars are huge and only shine for a short time.

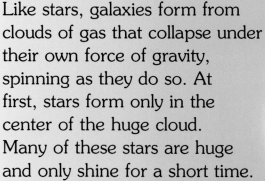

2 SPEEDS UP

Later, stars start to form in outer regions. As the young galaxy spins, matter around the central region begins to flatten into a disk. Globular clusters form from gas left over around the galaxy.

MILLIONS OF GALAXIES

Our galaxy is one of many in the universe. Pictures from the Hubble Space Telescope reveal that in every direction the Telescope can look, there are millions of galaxies to be seen (*below*). Because light takes so long to reach us from the farthest of these galaxies, they appear to us as they were when the universe was much younger.

3 NOW

The disk is now very pronounced, and spiral-shaped arms begin to form in it. Because matter is less dense within the spiral arms, star formation happens more slowly in these regions.

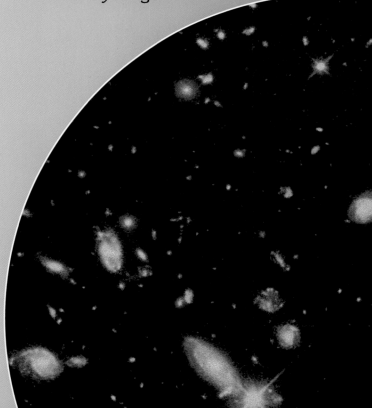

ACTIVE GALAXIES

We can see stars and galaxies because they give out visible light. However, many of them also emit invisible forms of radiation, such as X rays and radio waves. Active galaxies are powerful sources of these invisible forms of radiation. Astronomers believe that the power sources behind these active galaxies are massive black holes that spew out bursts of X rays and radio waves as they suck in huge amounts of matter.

RADIO GALAXY

Astronomers can make images using radio signals that objects give off. Seen in such a radio image, Centaurus A has two large radio-signal-emitting lobes (*above*). These lobes are above and below the plane of the galaxy and are thought to be given off by gas jets (*see right*). These plumes are enormous — they are about 100 times larger than the galaxy itself — and they stretch over some 10 degrees of the sky when observed from earth — 20 times wider than the full moon!

X-RAY GALAXY

When astronomers look at Centaurus A using X rays (*below*), they see areas that give off X rays on one side of the galaxy's core in the same direction as one of the radio wave lobes. These X rays are thought to be given off by charged particles moving in the magnetic field created by the galaxy.

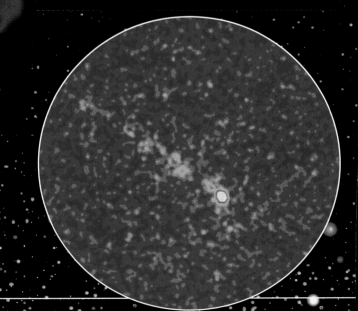

JETS FROM DARKNESS

The jets of gas ejected by the black hole escape in two huge plumes above and below the galaxy's center. After they have escaped, the gas particles slow down when they collide with other particles of gas and dust that surround the galaxy. These collisions warm the gas particles up to such a degree that they start to emit radio waves.

CENTAURUS A

The galaxy known as Centaurus A, which lies 17 million light-years from our own galaxy, is a powerful source of radiation. Photographic images of Centaurus A (*left*) show it as a very large, elliptical galaxy. At the center, astronomers believe a huge disk of gas is spinning around a black hole. This black hole is throwing out huge jets of gas in opposite directions at very high speeds — up to one-fifth of the speed of light (*below*).

BLACK HOLE POWER

The power behind some active galaxies is thought to be generated by huge black holes at their centers. These spinning black holes, with masses many, many thousands of times greater than the mass of the sun, suck in matter that, as it accelerates closer and closer to the hole, gives off the jets of gas (*see above*).

Black hole at the center of an active galaxy

GALAXY SHAPES

Not all galaxies are the same shape. The Milky Way, the Andromeda galaxy (*see* page 28), and the galaxy M100 (*right*) are spiral galaxies, the most common shape of galaxy. They have a central bulge region from which arms spiral out to form a swirling pattern. Other galaxy shapes are barred spiral, elliptical, and irregular.

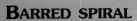

BARRED SPIRAL

This type of galaxy has a central bulge region with a bar-shaped structure running through it (*above*). From the ends of this bar, huge arms of stars spiral off. This shape of galaxy makes up about one-third of all the spiral galaxies.

IRREGULAR GALAXIES

Irregular galaxies, like this distant one spotted by the Hubble Space Telescope (*left*), have no regular structure to them. They make up one-fourth of all galaxies, and some of them are small, with just a few million stars.

ELLIPTICAL GALAXY

Elliptical galaxies are regular-shaped galaxies that do not have any signs of a spiral or a bar (*left*). They range from almost round in shape to flattened ovals. Some elliptical galaxies are huge, measuring several hundred millions of light-years from side to side and contain trillions of stars. These galaxies are very old and were formed within a billion years of the Big Bang (*see* pages 36-37).

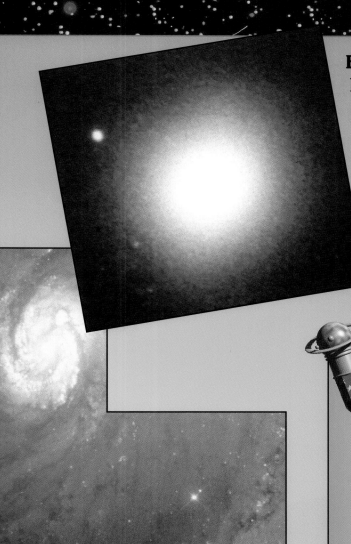

MAKE A SPIRAL

You can make a spiral shape on a piece of paper. Cut out a round-shaped piece of paper and ask an adult to pierce the center with a sharp pencil. With the pencil still in place, make sure that the paper will spin. Then drop some runny paint onto the center and spin the paper quickly. The paint will trail out from the center, forming spiral-shaped arms (*right*).

COLLISION COURSE

When two galaxies get close, their own gravity fields begin to distort them, pulling them out of shape. The curious shape of the Cartwheel galaxy (*left*) was caused by two galaxies colliding. When two galaxies collide, the stars within the galaxies do not actually hit each other, because the gaps between them are so huge.

GROUPS OF GALAXIES

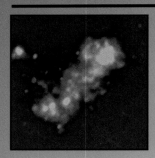

Just as stars group together into clusters and galaxies, so galaxies clump together into larger groups. Astronomers have found that these groups are, in turn, linked to other groups to form clusters that are also grouped in enormous structures — superclusters — that can measure millions of light-years across.

Andromeda

Triangulum galaxy

Milky Way

Milky Way

OUR GALAXY

The Milky Way (*above*) is so large that it takes our sun 200 million years to complete one orbit around it!

LOCAL GROUP

Our galaxy is part of a larger group, called the Local Group (*left*). This contains the Andromeda and Triangulum galaxies and 30 other minor galaxies, including the Small Magellanic Cloud (*top left*).

CLUSTERS OF GALAXIES

The Local Group, containing the Milky Way, is part of a much larger structure called a cluster. These clusters can contain thousands of galaxies. Our own cluster is known as the Canes Venatici cloud (*right*). Another, nearby cluster, the Virgo cluster (named Virgo because it is in the same part of the sky as the constellation of Virgo), contains about 1,000 galaxies and lies 50 million light-years away.

OUR UNIVERSE

From detailed surveys of the night sky, astronomers have found that there are billions of galaxies scattered in every direction (*above*). What they have also discovered is that these galaxies appear to be moving away from each other, sometimes at terrific speeds (*see* pages 36-37).

SUPERCLUSTERS

Clusters of galaxies are often linked with other clusters to form what are known as superclusters. The Local Group is at the edge of the Local Supercluster (*below*). Superclusters are usually made up of between three and ten clusters, and can be as much as 200 million light-years across.

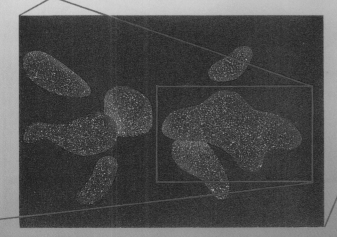

VOIDS IN SPACE

Astronomers have discovered that there are vast areas between superclusters that have nothing much in them, making up so-called voids (*above*). Surveys of the sky have shown that clusters tend to be found in large planes or curves with these empty spaces in between them. These voids are enormous — those found around our own supercluster are about 360 million light-years across!

START AND END

Scientists first developed the Big Bang theory after they discovered that all objects in space appear to be moving away from one another. This implies that the universe was much smaller than it is today. Astronomers are still looking for evidence to support this theory and for clues to how the universe might end.

ECHOES OF THE BANG
Evidence to support the Big Bang theory comes from this image (*above*). It shows the background temperature of the universe — the purple areas are slightly warmer than the blue. This uneven spread of temperature across the sky explains why matter clumped together to form the stars and galaxies after the Big Bang.

EXPANDING SPACE
Stick two stars to the surface of a balloon and blow it up (*below*). As the balloon inflates, the stars get farther apart. The gaps between objects in space are getting bigger, but the objects stay much the same size.

Big Bang

Present day

Universe expands from Big Bang.

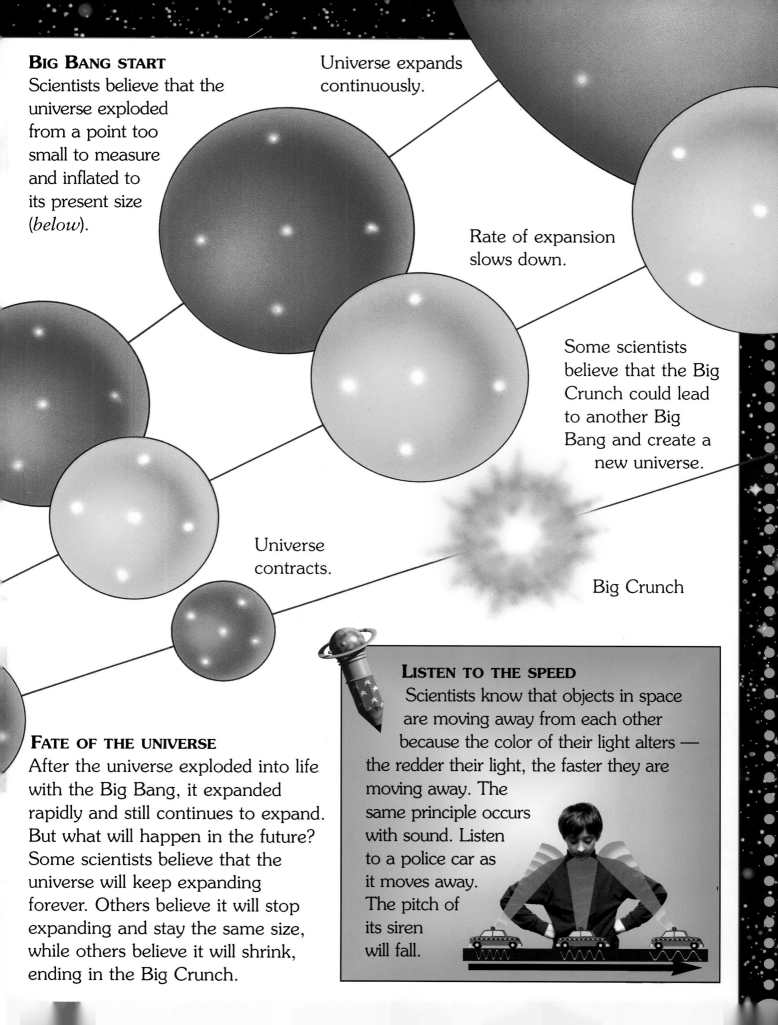

BIG BANG START
Scientists believe that the universe exploded from a point too small to measure and inflated to its present size (*below*).

Universe expands continuously.

Rate of expansion slows down.

Some scientists believe that the Big Crunch could lead to another Big Bang and create a new universe.

Universe contracts.

Big Crunch

FATE OF THE UNIVERSE
After the universe exploded into life with the Big Bang, it expanded rapidly and still continues to expand. But what will happen in the future? Some scientists believe that the universe will keep expanding forever. Others believe it will stop expanding and stay the same size, while others believe it will shrink, ending in the Big Crunch.

LISTEN TO THE SPEED
Scientists know that objects in space are moving away from each other because the color of their light alters — the redder their light, the faster they are moving away. The same principle occurs with sound. Listen to a police car as it moves away. The pitch of its siren will fall.

GLOSSARY

Absolute magnitude
This is the actual light output of an object. Absolute magnitudes compare the light output of stars as if they were seen from the same distance.

Active galaxies
These are galaxies that emit huge amounts of radiation, including radio waves and X rays. Astronomers believe that black holes are the cause of these powerful bursts of radiation.

Apparent magnitude
An object's brightness as it appears in the sky.

Big Bang
The theory that the universe began with an explosion of dense matter.

Black holes
The remains of massive stars that have exploded and collapsed in on themselves. The gravity is so strong that not even light can escape.

Bok globules
These are concentrations of gas and dust within nebulae. These denser areas collapse under the force of their own gravity until they ignite to form new stars.

Clusters
When stars or galaxies are grouped together, they are known as clusters. Star clusters are either open clusters, which are found inside galaxies, or globular clusters, which are found around the edges of galaxies.

Constellation
A collection of stars that have been grouped together in the night sky. Constellations are usually named after gods, heroes, or animals from ancient tales and myths.

Electromagnetic spectrum
The entire range of radiation, ranging from radio waves to gamma rays. It also includes all the colors of visible light and the invisible forms of radiation, such as infrared and ultraviolet light, as well as X rays and microwaves.

Galaxies
An enormous cluster of stars. Each galaxy can contain many billions of stars. Galaxies are classified as spiral, barred spiral, elliptical, or irregular. Our own galaxy is a spiral-shaped galaxy called the Milky Way. It contains as many as 100 billion stars.

Gravity

Every object in the universe has a force that attracts it to every other object. This force is called gravity. The larger or more dense the object, the greater its gravitational force. A large and very dense object, such as the sun, will have a higher gravitational force than a smaller, less dense object, such as the earth.

Hertzsprung-Russell diagram

A chart that compares the colors of stars with their surface temperatures, absolute magnitudes, sizes, and spectral types.

Light-years

Units used to measure distances in space. One light-year is the distance that a beam of light will travel in a year. This is equivalent to 5.9 million million miles (9.6 million million km).

Milky Way

The galaxy that contains our sun. It is called the Milky Way because it appears as a milky band that runs across the night sky.

Nebulae

These are huge clouds of gas that float around in space. They may be thousands of light-years across. Many nebulae are the remains of stars thrown off during an explosion, or nova.

Neutron stars

These are the remains of stars left after a massive star explosion, or supernova. These stars are made up of very tightly packed dense matter, and they emit powerful beams of radio waves that sweep the sky as the neutron star spins around.

Nuclear fusion

The process by which atoms are squeezed together and fused under high pressures and temperatures. This process gives out enormous amounts of energy, causing stars to shine.

Stars

Objects that generate enormous amounts of heat and light. They do this by squashing together the gas particles that make them up, in a process called nuclear fusion.

Sunspots

These are regions of the sun's surface, or photosphere, that are fractionally cooler and darker than the rest of the surface.

INDEX

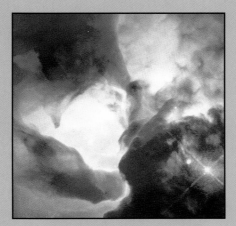

Photo credits:
Abbreviations: t-top, m-middle, b-bottom, r-right, l-left, c-center

All the photography in this book is provided by NASA except the following pages:
3r, 4t, 5b, 7t, 9, 13, 14, 19b, 21b, 22b, 23, 27b, 36b, 37, & 39br — Roger Vlitos. 4m — Pictor International. 4b, 6, & 38 both — Solution Pictures. 5m — United States Department of Agriculture. 25 both, 28t, 30 both, 31, & 36t — Science Photo Library.